SOCCER COACHES UNIVERSITY

- THE COACHING FILES VOLUME 1 -

Authors:

Mark Higginbotham & Eric Vogel

www.coachestrainingroom.com

Book cover design by GCreative.
Printed in the United States of America.

ISBN-13: 978-1721136032

ISBN-10: 1721136037

Special discounts available for bulk orders
(minimum of 30 copies)
Please email: info@coachestrainingroom.com

Dedication

This book is dedicated to the many hard working and passionate soccer coaches in the world and those who jumped in to be a coach because no one else would.

"I am a coach because of the kids and the passion I have for the sport itself. There is no other feeling quite like helping young athletes further develop their natural persistence, determination, discipline, dedication, resilience, work ethic, heart, leadership skills, connection with, and respect for others, not only in competition, but in life!"

-Coach Mahoe

www.coachestrainingroom.com

Table of Contents

Passing 21

Attacking/Dribbling 49

Movement and Field Usage

Using Support to Bypass Defenders

Dribbling - Carrying the ball forward.

Committing Defenders - Creating Space

Month 10 Dribbling - Identifying Space/Decision Making

Attack vs Defense - Problem Solving- Attack vs Defense

Attack vs Defense- Problem Solving - Attack vs Defense

The game of soccer is one of the fastest developing sports in the world, and with more technology and better practices more readily available than ever it is important to set yourself apart as a coach and as a team by staying at the forefront of modern coaching.

Effective learning requires exposure to real game situations. For example, you can practice passing in pairs 1000 times over and master the technique of passing and receiving to feet, but the techniques in soccer are never closed techniques; the ball you will have to control in a game will never be the same twice, and this is why it is important to practice the technique in a controlled and conditioned environment so that your players are fully prepared on game day.

Inside this guide you will find full session plans designed to develop confidence and ability by conditioning the learning into conditioned and scalable, real game scenarios.

We believe there are 1000's of ways to arrive at the same destination, which is why you will find linked sessions, progressions and alternatives all within this guide so that your players can practice what they have learned under a different set of conditions to help them not only remember what they have practiced, but also understand why they're practicing this way, allowing for greater information retention and understanding.

Each full session is broken down into a warm up/isolated technique, technique under passive pressure, a real pressure scenario followed by a conditioned small sided game.

In this guide you will be provided with a collection of balanced and scalable game based training sessions and small sided games. Set in an easily digestible format designed to maximize the player development in your sessions.

Defending

Considerations

- Basic defensive technique- sideways stance, even balance, force the attacker in one direction

- Your role within the defensive unit

- Principles of the first defender - Delay, direction, patience.

- Principles of the second defender - Depth, space, awareness, reactions

- Principles of the third defender - Compactness, awareness, reactions to field developments, cutting out passing angles, field balance.

Individual Technique and Positioning

SCU Online Reference:
Month 2 Defending

Musical Chairs

How To: Set out a 35 x 35-yard area with an equal number of cones to the number of players you have. Spread the cones randomly throughout the area. Players simulate in-game movements as a warm-up (jumping to head the ball, jockeying for the ball, sprints, quick changes of direction etc). When coach signals, players must move quickly to a cone and assume a defensive stance (1 player per cone). After each round, remove a cone and create a quick elimination game.

Coaching Points: Defensive positioning: side on, even weight distribution, low center of gravity, touch tight. Knowing your surroundings, reaction times.

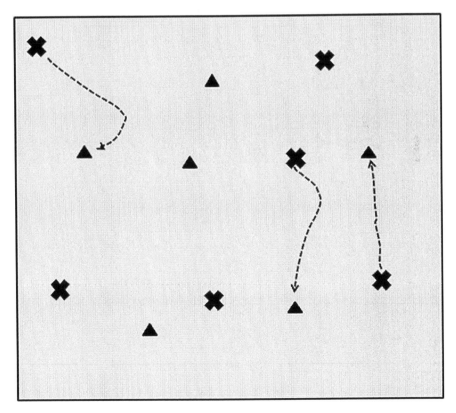

Month 2-2

1v1 Defending the Advancing Attacker

How To: set up two 12 x 12-yard area inside a 35 x 35-yard area. A start line at one side and a Pop-Up Goal at the other end. 1 defender in each area. Attackers must dribble into the area and attempt to exit the other side of the square before shooting on goal. Defenders must try to force players outside either side of the square and not allow the attacker to pass them.

Coaching Points: This game should be played at half speed. Attackers should allow the defender to practice proper form by approaching at half speed then slowly building up to full speed. The proper approach, get touch tight, make play predictable.

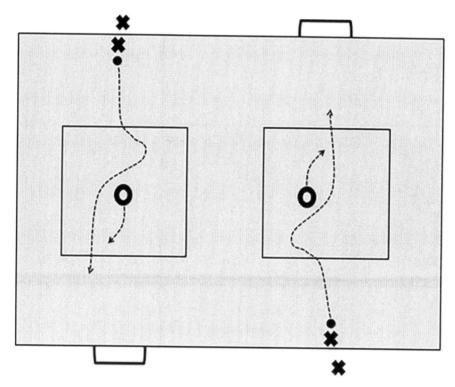

Defending the Cone

How To: 20 x 20-yard square with a 3 x 3-yard area in the middle. Place a cone/target in this central area (a ball on top of a cone works perfectly). One defender occupies the middle space with 3 or 4 players around the outside. Outside players must work opportunities to take a shot at the target and knock it over. The defender must move to block all attempts without entering the central area where the ball is.

Coaching Points: Defender must move their position quickly to cut off angles and restrict opportunities. Anticipate play and change direction quickly to prevent attacks, determination and hard work are key ingredients for success here.

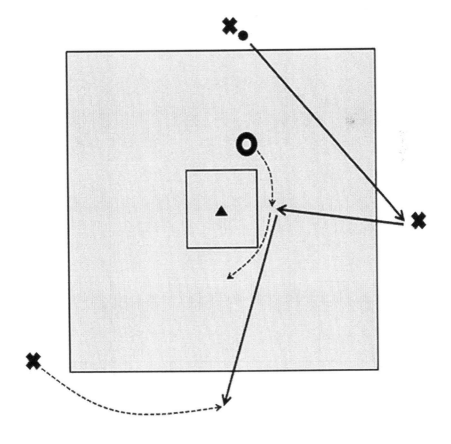

Opposite Numbers- Man Marking SSG

How To: Set up two even teams and number each player. Each player has an opposite number on the opposing team. Player 1 Yellow can only challenge player 1 red for the ball and vice versa. This is a conditioned Man-Marking game designed to encourage 1v1's and losing your marker. Focus on the attacking coaching points, you can always revisit it from a defensive perspective another time.

Coaching Points: Know your surroundings, keep an eye on your opposite player when you don't have the ball. Track runs and restrict space. When in possession, move quickly to lose your marker, use space when it becomes available. Communicate with teammates constantly. Be positive when you have the ball and take your player on when possible, be creative.

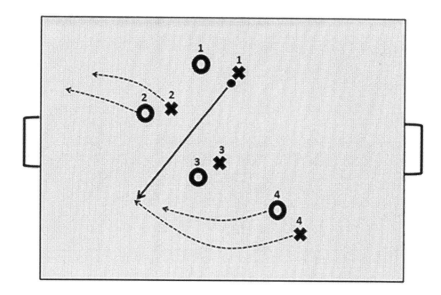

Month 2-1A

Find a Friend (Alternative 1)

How To: Set up two teams in two different colored bibs. Each player should partner up with a player wearing a different colored bib to themselves. Players simulate in-game movements as a warm-up (jumping to head the ball, jockeying for the ball, sprints, quick changes of direction etc.) When coach signals the players must find their partner and move quickly to them, stopping next to each other to signal they're done.

Key Differences: Focus has gone from looking at still objects on the ground to finding a moving target, developing field awareness and reaction skills, players will be keeping their heads up naturally.

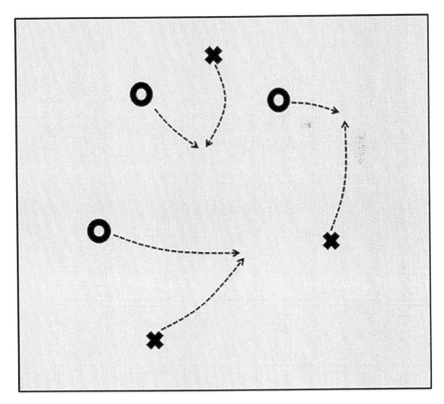

1v1 Defend and Counter (Alternative 2)

How To: set up two 12 x 12-yard area inside a 35 x 35-yard area. A start line at one side and a Pop-Up Goal at both ends. 1 defender in each area. Attackers must dribble into the area and attempt to exit the other side of the square before shooting on goal. Defenders must try to win the ball back before mounting a counter-attack of their own and scoring in the pop-up goal opposite.

Key differences: Defensive approach technique; make play predictable, be patient and disciplined. Wait for the opportunity to win the ball back. **This session should come as a progression to <u>1v1 Defending the advancing attacker.</u>** The defender should be positive with their next move in mind if they do win possession back, this encourages calm play once possession is regained and stops players from making blind clearances.

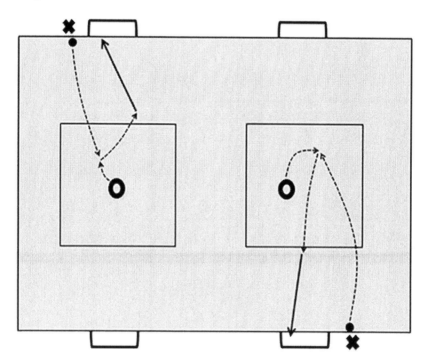

Defensive Screening (Alternative 3)

How To: Set up a 35 x 30-yard area played width ways. Set out an internal 5-yard channel down the full width of the field as shown, Defenders occupy the central area with passing teams at either side. The possession team must pass to each other working space to pass the ball on the ground through the defenders. The score a point for every successful pass through the defenders.

Key Differences: Defenders must be aware of the field and how possession is developing, Targets are now moving so they must be able to watch play continuously and react accordingly.

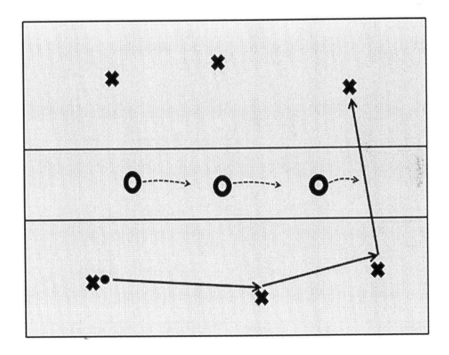

Opposite Numbers- Man Marking SSG (3 touch min) (Alternative 4)

How To: Set up two even teams and number each player. Each player has an opposite number on the opposing team. Player 1 Yellow can only challenge player 1 red for the ball and vice versa. This is a conditioned Man-Marking game. **The Player in possession must make a minimum of 3 touches on the ball before passing.**

Key Differences: The player will have to remain in possession for longer giving the opposite number longer to recover and focus on defensive form. It also encourages players to take a touch and get their head up to view the field.

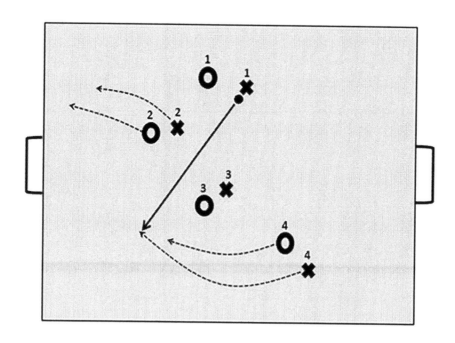

Organization and Structure

SCU Online Reference:
Month 8 Defending

Defending 1v1 – Areas of the Field

How To: Using half a field set up 15 x 10-yard areas across the field, 1v1 is played in each zone, the defender starts the game by passing into the attacker.

Coaching Points: Look at where you are on the field, if you're playing 1v1 on the outside usher attacker away from goal, if you're defending in a central zone force the attacker away from goal and remain between ball and goal, be patient and slow the attack down. Remain side on and keep a low center of gravity, remain on your toes and make play predictable. Rotate the zones regularly so players can get used to defending in different areas of the field, for example, if they're defending the left side of the field they may need to lead with the right foot in order to send the attacker towards the sideline.

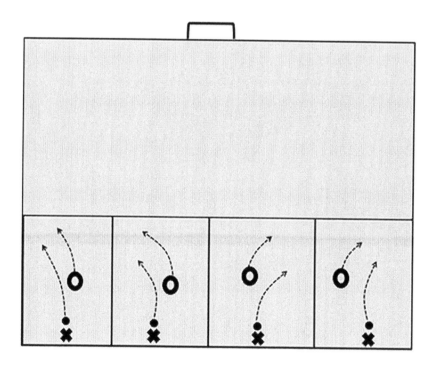

Defending 2v2 – Delaying and Communication

How To: Continuing from the 1v1 field set up, remove two of the lines forming two larger areas. Defender passes the ball into the attackers to set up a 2v2. If the attackers can bypass the defenders they can take a shot on goal and score a point. If the defenders can win the ball back they can dribble over the end line and score a point.

Coaching Points: Communication and discipline to identify your role in the defensive unit and play it. One player pressures the ball quickly, the secondary defender provides depth and cover and also monitors the movement of the second attacker and reacts accordingly.

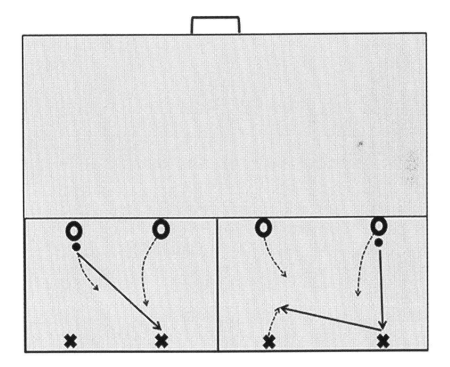

Overloads

How To: Set up a 5v4 in the attackers' favor with 2 deeper lying unopposed attackers making a 7v4. Defenders must work as a unit to repel the attacks.

Coaching Points: Communication and organization are crucial, change roles with the movement of the ball and move with the defensive unit. Track runners and assess the danger. You are outnumbered, focus on the immediate danger and identify threats from there. Try to repel the attack for as long as possible. A well-organized defense can still repel an overloaded attack.

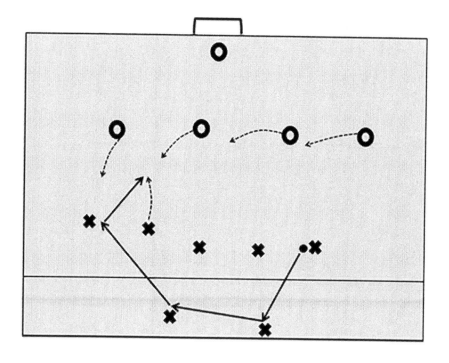

Ringing Changes SSG

How To: Play a 4v4 small-sided game under normal game rules. One team waits on the sideline. Once a team concedes they must quickly leave the field and the waiting team must come on in their place. Winner stays on.

Coaching Points: Defensive technique both individually and part of a team. Try to remain in play for as long as possible. Communicate and remember your roles. Defensive principles of delaying, depth, concentration and discipline.

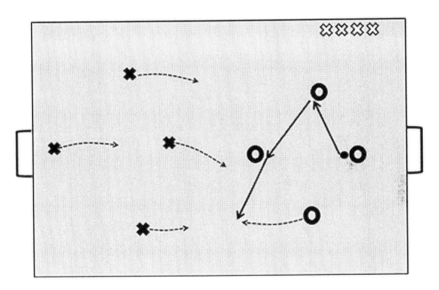

60 - 40%'s

How To: Using half a field set up 15 x 10-yard areas across the field, 1v1 is played in each zone, the ball starts in the middle slightly closer to the attacker and players start at the same time.

Key Differences: The ball is closer to the attacker and they should get to the ball first. It encourages the defender to press quickly and deny the space. Encourage getting touch tight (Arm's length) from the attacker and maintaining a good defensive position. Show the attacker to one area of the field.

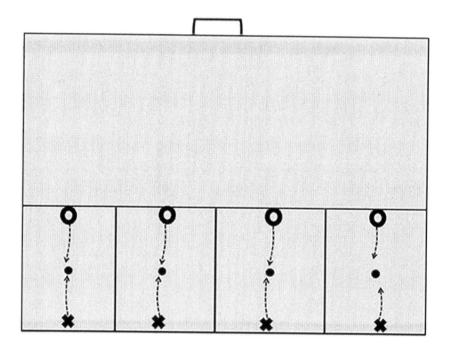

Defending 2v2 – Quick Press.

How To: The attackers start with the ball and start their attack immediately. The defenders cannot move until the attacker touches the ball. They must press quickly and play 2v2. The attackers can shoot on goal if they're able to dribble over the end line.

Key Differences: Since the attacker starts with the ball the defenders must be alert and ready to press the attackers quickly. Try to close down the attackers as far from the goal as you can to give yourselves chance to defend as far away from your own goal as possible. Be careful not to over-commit.

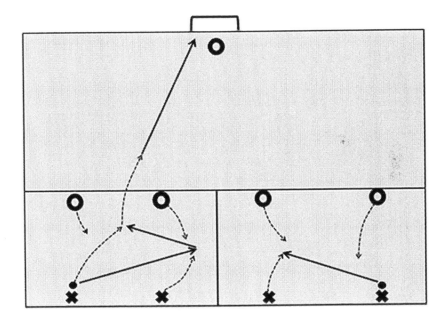

3v3

How To: Remove the central line and increase the length of the square to 25 yards. The defender feeds the ball into any of the 3 attackers and the teams play 3v3. Attackers can shoot on the goal if they win possession. Defenders can dribble over the attacking end line if they win the ball back.

Key Differences: Extra defender will add a different role. The third defender must provide balance to the defense by cutting off passing angles, watching the play develop and providing cover for the second defender. This will give a more realistic game feel.

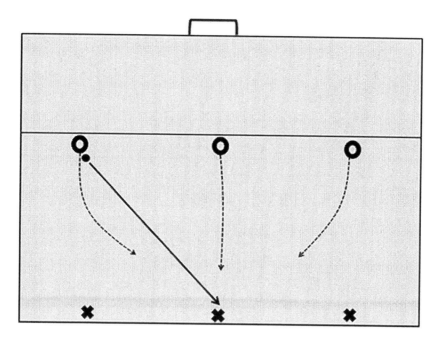

SSG – Defensive Emphasis.

How To: Play a 4v4 small-sided game under normal game rules.

Coaching Points: Defensive technique both individually and part of a team. As the coach, feel free to use your whistle to "freeze" the players on the spot so you can deliver coaching points and ask questions. Remember roles as a defensive unit. Provide cover, communicate, pressure the attackers and encourage each other. Praise good defensive work individually and as a team.

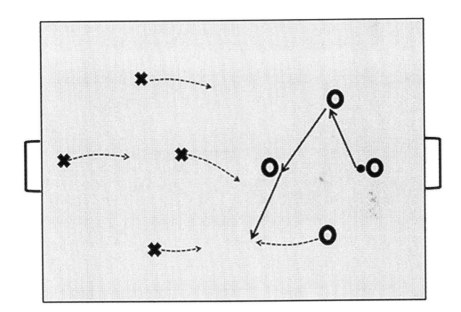

Passing

Considerations

- Space and surroundings, look for the extra player
- Try to view the field as a number of smaller sided games (1v1, 2v2, react to create overloads 3v2 etc.)
- Identify opportunities and threats

Type of Pass:

- Pass to feet- technique and accuracy
- Pass to space - weight, timing and awareness
- Cut pass - hips square, pass played on an angle 'around the corner' into the diagonal pocket
- Chipped/lofted passes- Weight of pass, technique and accuracy

Playing Out From the Back

SCU Online Reference:
Month 9 Passing

Passing out from the Back - Patterns

How To: Set up a 15 x 15-yard diamond. With starting lines at either side and a player in the middle. 4 Players per area. The middle player moves to a free corner to receive a pass. The opposite player from the starting line moves to take the free space in the middle and receives a pass out wide on the half turn then plays a pass to the opposite end. The wide player moves to that end.

Coaching Points: Open out to the side quickly to create space for the pass. The dropping midfielder supports in the free space and moves the attack downfield. Receiving on the half turn gives a better view of the field and helps you play in the right direction. Composure, communication movement and passing technique are important for success.

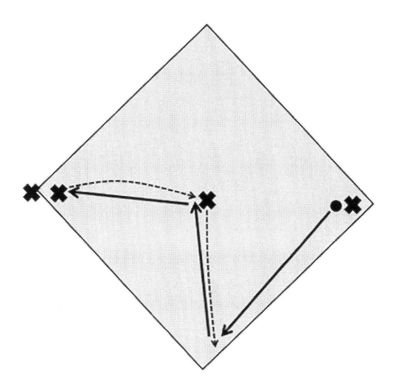

Playing out by Colors

How To: 45 x 30-yard field with two 5-yard channels. 2 outfield players in one color and 2 in another color. With the keeper in possession, the players with the same color bib as the goalkeeper push out wide to create space and the 4 outfield players work together to create a scoring opportunity. The pattern repeats from the other end.

Coaching Points: Communication, movement, teamwork to create the width and space to play out from the goalkeeper. Receive on the half turn and be confident in possession. Composure is crucial when playing out from defense, constant support, first touch and passing accuracy are essential.

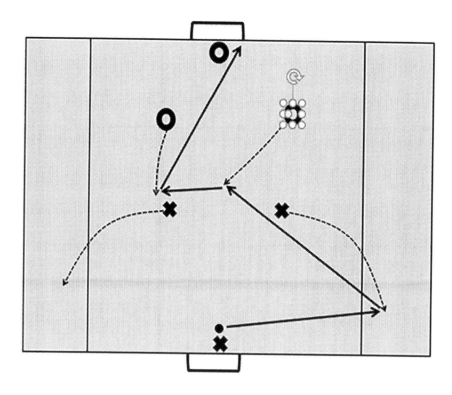

Playing out by Colors 4v2

How To: Using the 45 x 30-yard area, set out a halfway line. Play 4 v 2 from the goalkeeper. Players moving to a wide area to receive the ball cannot be challenged but can only stay out wide in the channel for 3 seconds.

Coaching Points: Create width to create space to play the ball. Support your teammates and use the goalkeeper to switch the play to the other side when necessary. Do not pass directly across your own goal. Watch the field develop and occupy space to support. Move the ball quickly and remain composed. Identify when to pass to feet and when to pass to space.

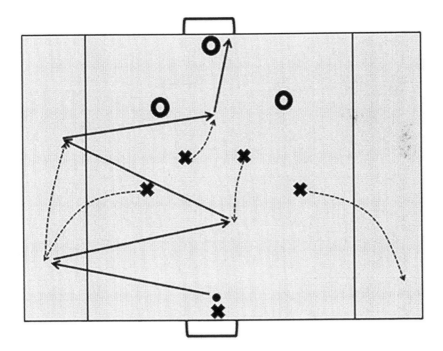

Playing out from the back SSG

How To: Play a 4v4 small-sided game under normal game rules. The side channels can only be occupied by the team in possession so this is an area to receive the ball unopposed. Players can only occupy this area for 3 seconds. And cannot re-enter for 5 seconds after exiting. The ball must be passed out from the back and any break in play always restarts with the goalkeeper.

Coaching Points: Composure and confidence to receive the pass and play the next ball. Don't be afraid to make mistakes, they happen. Passing accuracy, movement and identification of space and passing opportunities, play with your head up and be positive. Move the ball quickly and focus on technique at all times.

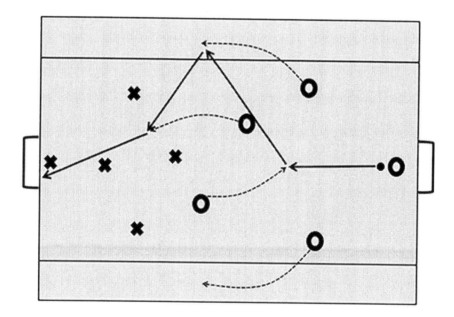

Passing out from the Back – Patterns

How To: Set up a 15 x 15-yard diamond. With starting lines at either side and a player in the middle. 4 Players per area. The middle player moves to a free corner to receive a pass. The opposite player from the starting line moves to take the free space in the middle and receives a pass out wide on the half turn then plays a pass to the opposite end. The wide player moves to that end.

Key Differences: The defender opens out wide to create space for the dropping midfielder to receive the pass down the middle. The pass from the midfielder should be played as a pivot player, moving the wide player on to attack the space by passing in front of them.

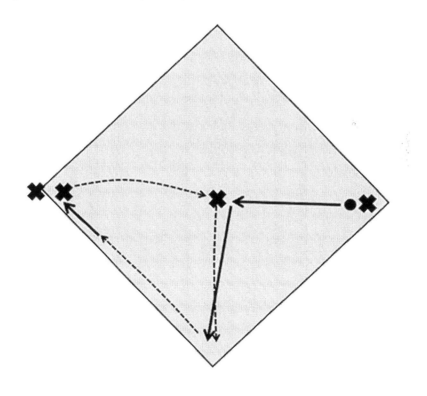

Playing out by Colors

How To: 45 x 30-yard field with two 5-yard channels. 2 outfield players in one color and 2 in another color. With the keeper in possession, the players with the same color bib as the goalkeeper push out wide to create space and the 4 outfield players work together to create a scoring opportunity. The pattern repeats from the other end.

Key Differences: The ball must pass through 3 sides of the inner area (1 being the shot) Players must drop to receive and open out wide to create space and passing opportunities. Passing the ball through 2 sides in one pass does not count. Moves should be fluid motions. Passing accuracy and first touch are vital to keeping the play moving.

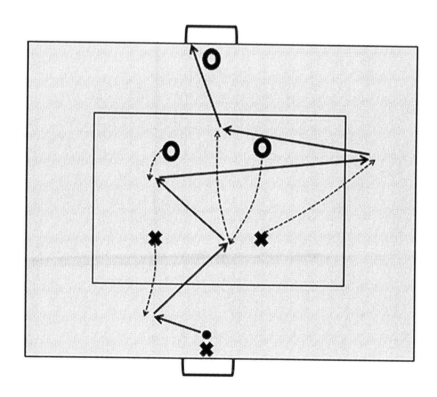

Month 9-3A

Playing Out by Colors 4v2

How To: Using the 45 x 30-yard area, set out a halfway line. Play 4 v 2 from the goalkeeper. The ball must be dribbled over the middle line before shooting. Play starts with the goalkeeper who started originally.

Key Differences: No safe areas on the field. This means players are under more pressure in possession and must look for the simple support pass. Create gaps in the opposition by moving the ball quickly and attack space when you have made it.

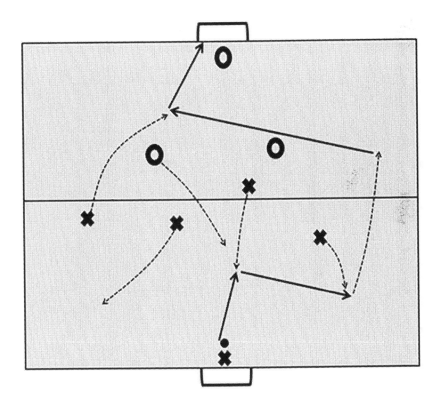

Playing Out from The Back SSG

How To: Play a 4v4 small-sided game under normal game rules. The ball must be dribbled over the halfway line when building an attack.

Key Differences: No safe zones. As a Coach, you have a choice whether to limit the number of opponents that can enter the other half when not in possession. There are no safe zones so you can build the pressure as you wish. You can create full pressure high press situations by allowing all 4 players to close down the team playing out from the back but build this up in increments. This is beneficial from an attack and defense perspective.

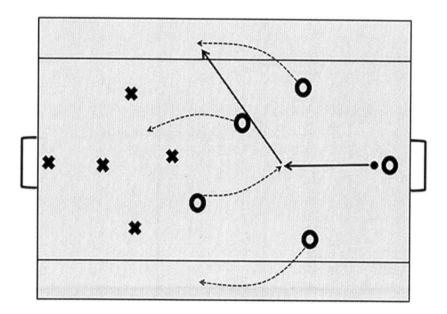

Field Awareness- Attacking Emphasis

SCU Online Reference:
Month 4 Passing

Passing Patterns Warm-up

How To: Set up a 10 x 10-yard square with a player on each cone. One player starts with a ball. The player passes to the player near the next cone and receives a return pass before making a final pass back to the player on the next cone, the pattern repeats. Each player stays around their starting cone.

Coaching Points: Pass on an angle, draw your teammate into the good space, lateral passes are predictable and easy to defend, using angles helps to move the play in the direction you want to be moving. Basic passing technique, communication and movement are all essential.

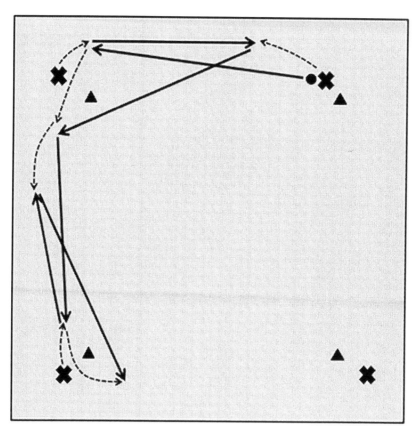

Movement and Awareness- Protect the Ball.

How To: Use a 10-yard diameter area with 4 players around the outside, two balls between 4. Place a ball in the center of the area, one player occupies the center area. One outside player with a ball must pass towards the cone the player in the middle must control the pass and play the ball out of the area to a free player. Once the free player receives the pass the next person with a ball must pass at the ball.

Coaching Points: Middle player works hard to control the pass and identify the available player, try to read the play so you know where you need to pass to before you receive the ball. Focus on a good first touch and accurate passes, quick thinking will allow for more time for movement.

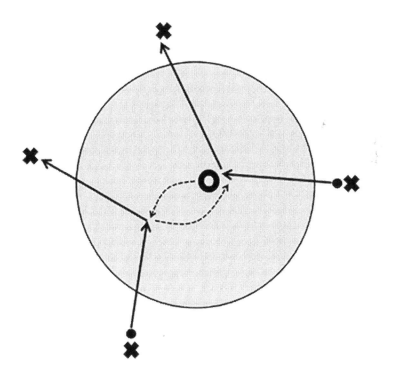

Diamond Passing and 1v1's

How To: Set up a large diamond approx. 30 yards from goal. Players start on each cone, pass and follow your pass as shown in the diagram. The player receiving the final pass with their back to goal must lay the ball off to the advancing attacker and become the defender playing a 1v1 to goal.

Coaching Points: Accuracy and technique when passing. Experiment with the layoff pass, adjust the angle it is played at, passing straight back to the attacker will give you time to defend on the front foot, a layoff on an angle will make life harder for the defender, try to think how this relates to a real game situation.

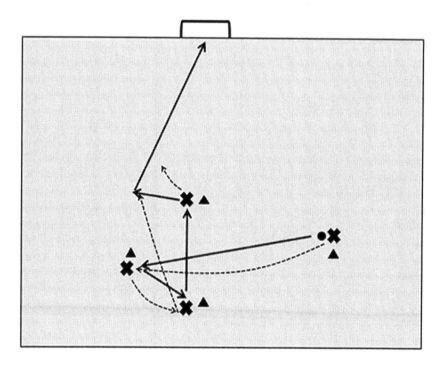

Attack and Defense Transitions SSG

How To: Set up two 20 x 25-yard fields next to each other with a goal at either end. Adapt the size of the field to accommodate 4v4 or 5v5, however, the speed of play is paramount so smaller numbers are better. The first team to score must collect the ball and attack the other goal, the team who conceded must run around the goal and attempt to win the ball back before the other team leaves the field. The defending team must set up to repel the attack and win the ball back and score.

Coaching Points: Create space, attack at speed, if you lose the ball try to win it back quickly. Communicate and work as a unit.

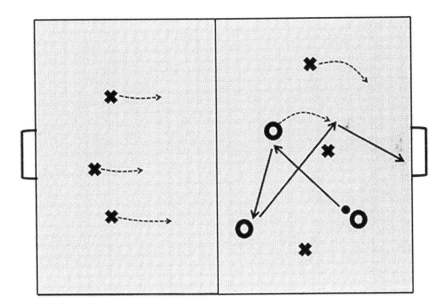

Passing Patterns - Alternative 1

How To: Set up a 10 x 10- yard square with a player on each cone. One player starts with a ball. The player passes to the player near the next cone and receives a return pass before making a final pass back to the player on the next cone, the pattern repeats. Each player stays around their starting cone.

Key Differences: Pass and move around the area, follow your pass on an angle and move your teammate into the right space by passing in front of them so they can naturally pass to the next player. Rather than maintaining your position you are advancing around the field so you must also consider your own run and timing.

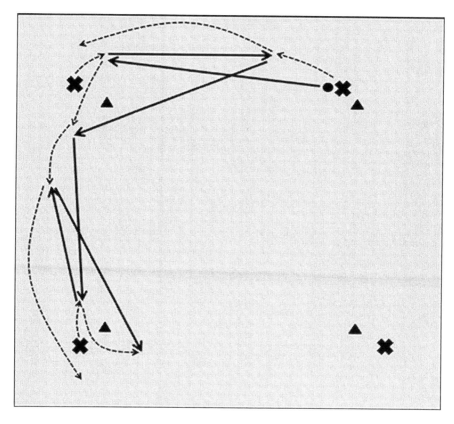

Movement and Creating Space Alternative 2

How To: Use a 10-yard diameter area with 4 players around the outside, two balls between 4. Place a ball in the center of the area, one player occupies the center area with one defender. One outside player with a ball must pass to the free player who then passes to a free player on the outside then moves to find the next player with a ball to receive a pass from.

Coaching Points: Defender is trying to win the ball back, defenders use half pressure initially so the receiving player can understand body position and begin natural correction of technique. Players will naturally use more of the area in this environment. The defender should always look to apply pressure on the player's first touch even at half speed to practice in game situations in a conditioned environment.

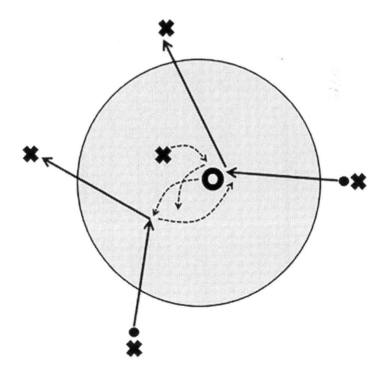

Diamond passing and 1v1's Alternative 3

How To: Set up a large diamond approx. 30 yards from goal. Players start on each cone, pass and follow your pass as shown in the diagram. The player receiving the final pass with their back to goal must pass directly into the body of the attacker before playing a 1v1.

Key Differences: Final pass is much more direct offering a very pure 1v1 scenario. The emphasis of angle on final pass is taken away, players will see the benefit of the final ball as they will now have a much more even 50/50 1v1

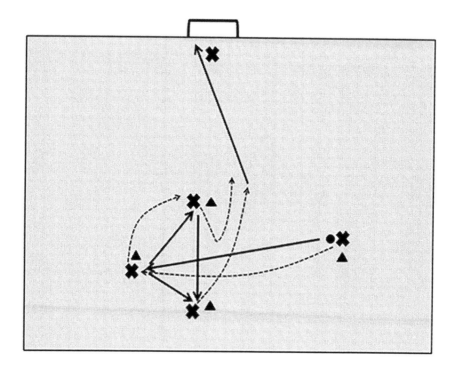

Attack and Defense Transitions SSG Alternative 4

How to: Set up two 20 x 25-yard fields next to each other with 2 goals at either end. Adapt the size of the field to accommodate 4v4 or 5v5, however, speed of play is paramount so smaller numbers are better. The first team to score must collect the ball and attack the other goal, the team who conceded must run around the goal and attempt to win the ball back before the other team leaves the field. The defending team must set up to repel the attack and win the ball back and score.

Key Differences: Extra goal creates more goal-scoring opportunities and therefore more transitions between attack and defense limiting waiting times and lessening a team's ability to set up an organized defense

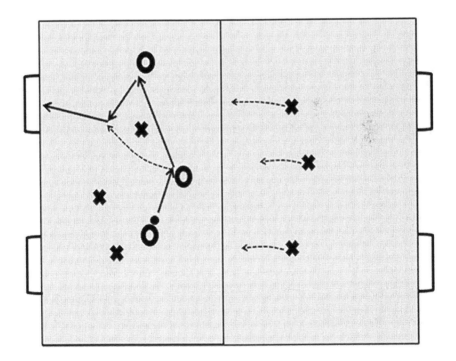

Creating Space - Dynamic Reactions

SCU Online Reference:
Month 6 Passing

Move and Move

Area: 8 x8 yard square with a cone in each corner and a cone in the middle. A player stands by each cone with 2 players on the starting cone. No Soccer balls are required for this warm up.

How To: A player from the start line runs to a player and tags them, the tagged player must then run and tag another player on another cone. The pattern continues until coach calls time.

Coaching Points: Move quickly and watch the field develop, have an idea of where you will run to before you get tagged so that your movement is automatic. You are reacting to other people's movement at all times so remain alert.

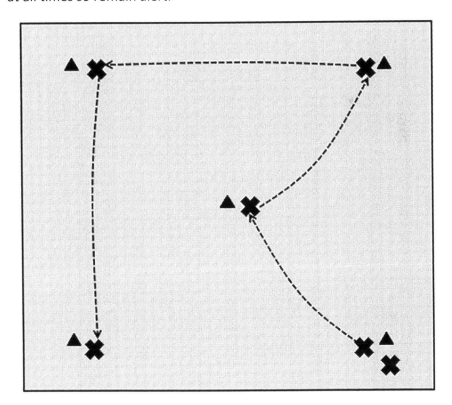

Movement off Movement

How To: set up 3 lines 45 yards away from goal. The keeper starts with the ball and passes to the wide player 1. Player 3 moves in field to collect a pass from player 1 and player 2 moves out wide to occupy the space created by player 3. Player 3 passes to player 2 out wide and continues a run into space in the channel player 1 occupies. Player one moves into the vacated space and plays a 1-2 with player 2 who shoots on goal.

Coaching Points: Imagine the field is divided into 3 channels, only one player should occupy 1 channel at any one time (place coned channels to help players visually at first if necessary.). Scan your surroundings and communicate. Try to make the movement downfield and in and out of channels as fluid as possible, this will require communication and understanding of your team-mates.

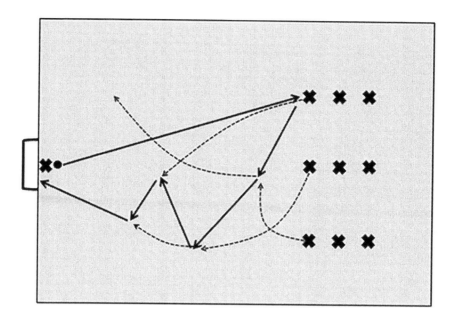

Movement- Numbers up: Practical Application

How To: Start with a ball in from the edge of the field (Pass or throw in) and play the ball into the player in the middle who then moves the ball out wide. The throw in taker moves infield and the middle-man moves into the space that the inside run creates. This is a 3v1 scenario

Coaching Points: The numbers up situation should allow the pattern to naturally free at least one player with their run. Focus on the pattern and how your own movement can put doubt into a defender. Blind-sided runs work to lose your defender, running across the face of the defender can lure them out of position.

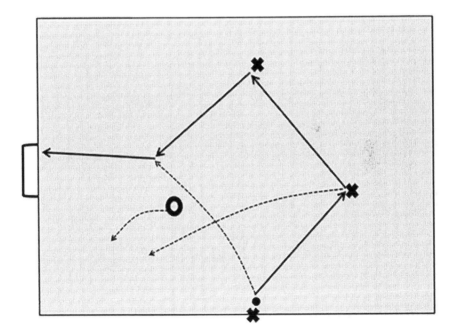

Jokers SSG

How To: 25 x 35-yard field with two small scoring zones at either end. Players play a 4v3 or 5v4 under normal game conditions. One player on the attacking team will be nominated as a Joker. They will be unable to touch the ball and can only influence the play with their movement. The identity of the joker is kept a secret from the opposition. After a goal is scored the defending team tries to guess the joker, if they are unable to identify the joker the goal counts as 2.

Coaching Points: Without good movement, this will be a simple even numbers game. It's vital that the Joker influences the game in any way possible. Moving into space, committing defenders, dropping deep to draw a defender out of position

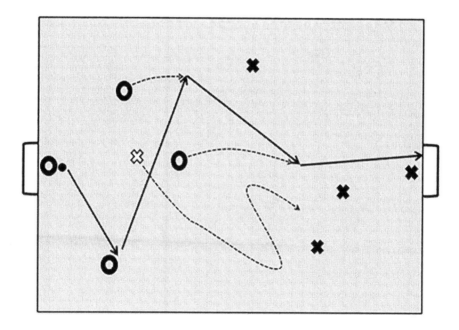

Pass and Move to Free Cone Alternative 1

How To: Use the 8 x 8-yard area used for Move and Move and use 4 players leaving one cone free. Players must pass to a free player and move to the free cone. This game should be played at speed but with accuracy.

Key Differences: Adding a ball adds the real-game scenario. The free cone will always move, you have to react to the pass and move quickly so your ability to watch the field and acknowledge the space before the ball is played to you will be tested.

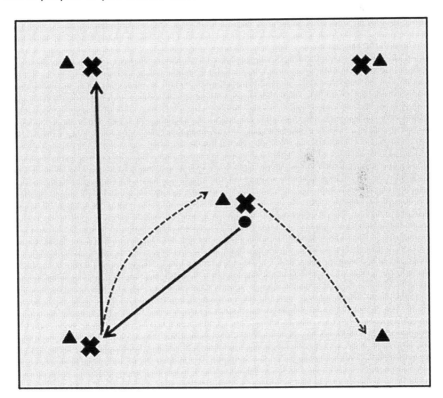

Movement off Movement- Numbers up- Advanced

How To: set up 3 lines 45 yards away from goal. The keeper starts with the ball and passes to any of the 3 players. The players can operate in free play, taking on the one defender before shooting on goal. There must be at least 2 lane switches between players.

Key Differences: Adding the defender will add some real but passive pressure. The players will have to use the understanding they were developing in a controlled environment under a more real-game scenario. Communication and quick, fluid movement will still be crucial in order to successfully bypass the defender.

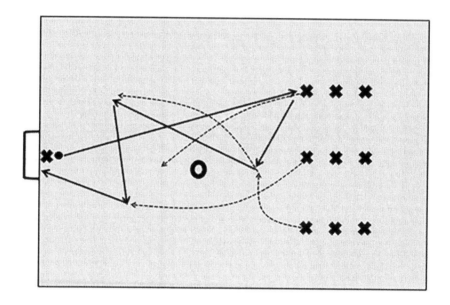

Movement- Numbers up:
Practical Application Advanced

How To: Start with a ball in from the edge of the field (Pass or throw in) and play the ball into the player in the middle who then moves the ball out wide. The throw in taker moves infield and the middleman moves into the space that the inside run creates. This is a 3v2 scenario.

Key Differences: The 3 v 2 makes the run of the spare man even more important. The aim is to draw a defender in with your movement to free up another player. Move the ball quicker and take advantage of overlapping/underlapping runs.

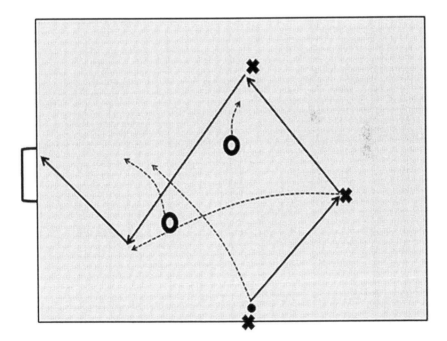

Jokers SSG

How To: 25 x 35-yard field with two small scoring zones at either end. Players play a 4v4 or 5v4 under normal game conditions. **One player on each team will be nominated as a Joker**. They will be unable to touch the ball and can only influence the play with their movement. The identity of the joker is kept a secret from the opposition. After a goal is scored the defending team try to guess the joker, if they are unable to identify the joker the goal counts as 2.

Key Differences: New jokers are nominated secretly after each goal. Jokers can challenge for the ball when defending. This is an even numbers game and should flow as naturally as possible. Joker runs should be varied and challenging for the opposition.

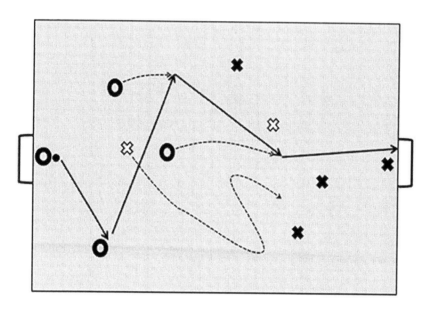

Attacking/Dribbling

Considerations

- Space, identification of opportunities and threats

- Reactions, positivity on the ball

- Basic shooting technique- Accuracy, head over the ball, cleverness of finish and composure.

- Retaining possession, shielding the ball

- Differences between dribbling and running with the ball.

- Dribbling a ball into space or dribbling at a defender to create space elsewhere

Methods of attack:

- Through the middle- accuracy, speed, use of spare man, the weight of pass, control

- Around the sides - Width, pace, isolating defenders, overloads/overlaps, delivery type.

- Over the top - long balls to a target player, positive runs off the target player for flick-ons.

Movement and Field Usage

SCU Online Reference:
Month 3 Attacking

Finding Space

How To: Set up an area with clearly marked zones, the area should be large to encourage conditioning and movement. Have more zones than there are players. Defenders must move themselves into the same zone as an attacker, attackers must move to zones that are free from defenders. Coach stops the game at intervals and the free space is discussed.

Coaching Points: 2 points scored if you're in a zone on your own, one point if you're in a zone with another attacker, 0 points if you're in a zone with a defender when the game stops. Scan the field, keep your head up and know your surroundings, you may not have to move to be in space, work cleverly and watch play develop.

Progressions: Include a soccer ball for all players including defenders.

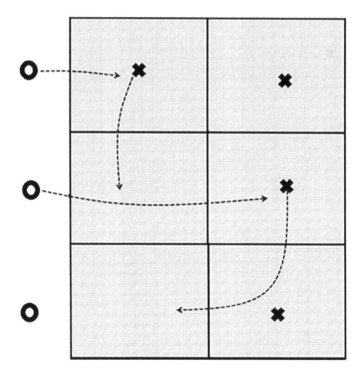

2v1 4 Goal Game

How To: Set up a 25 x 20-yard area with 4 PUG's at either end. Players start on opposite sides in the middle of the field. One defender passes the ball into either one of the two attackers. Attackers can score into any goal after making a minimum of 3 in field passes.

Coaching Points: Creativity, use the space available to move the defender, communicate with your team mate and manipulate the space in order to create scoring opportunities. Use trickery and fakes to commit the defender and open up the field for other opportunities.

Progressions:

- Cannot score in the same goal twice in a row.

- Cannot score on the same side twice in a row

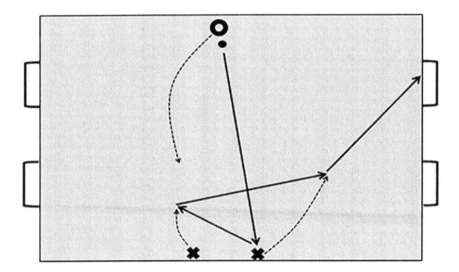

2v2 4 Goal Conditioned Game

How To: Set up a 25 x 20 yard area with 4 PUG's at either end. Players start on opposite sides in the middle of the field. One defender passes the ball into either one of the two attackers. Attackers can score into any goal after making a minimum of 3 in field passes.

Coaching Points: Movement, communication, field awareness and use of the field are all critical components for success, if the defenders win the ball they must make 3 passes and score.

Progressions:

- Set a time limit. Which team can make the most passes within that time limit before scoring?

- Cannot score on the same side twice in a row

This game is a progression for <u>2v1 4 Goal Game</u>

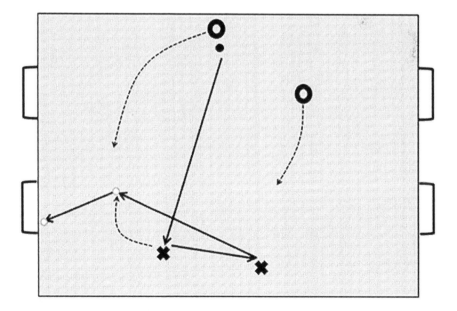

Back to Back Goal SSG

How To: Set up a 50 x 45-yard area with two goals placed back to back in the middle of the field. One team defends one, the other team defends the other. Normal game rules apply.

Coaching Points: Use space, spread out and create gaps, search for opportunities and exploit them, communicate and work on quick transitions from defense to attack and vice-versa. Attack and defend as a team. Be patient in build-up play and don't be afraid to rebuild an attack by switching the point of attack.

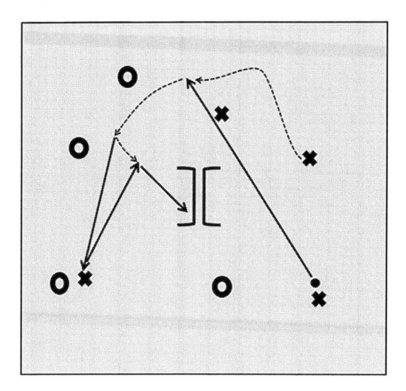

Abandon Ship (Alternative 1)

How To: Set up a team of players in one half of a field with a coned section down the middle, a defender occupies the middle section, players move unopposed in their half of the field, on the signal, the defender is released and can try to kick a players' ball out of the area, players must dribble to the other half of the field to safety. This should be played under no pressure for the first few rounds.

Key Differences: Players are now attempting to move past a player as they would do on a field, aiming for a final destination as opposed to choosing available field space

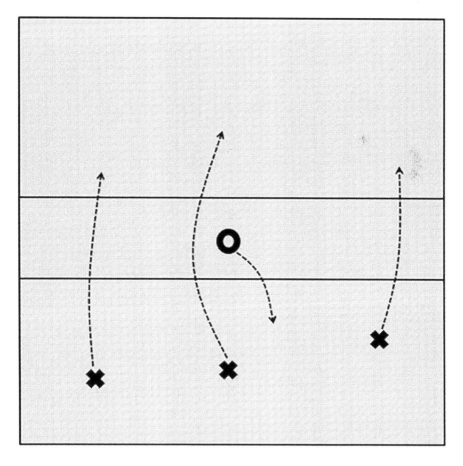

2v1 2 Goal Conditioned Game (Alternative 2)

How To: Set up a 25 x 20-yard area with a Pop Up Goal at either end. Players start on opposite sides in the middle of the field. One defender passes the ball into either one of the two attackers. Attackers can score into any goal after making a minimum of 3 in field passes. They must take their shot before the coned line shown

Key Differences: Scoring opportunities are limited and there is a greater emphasis on accuracy, players must show creativity to allow space for the accurate shot

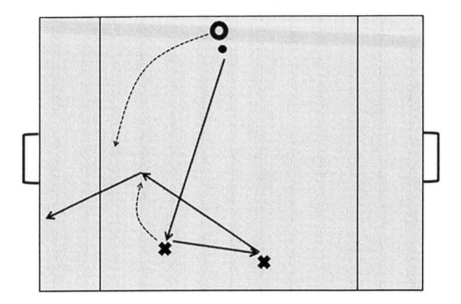

3v2 with Channels (Alternative 3)

How To: Set up a 35 x 30 yard area with 2 PUG's at either end and a coned channel down either side-line. Players start on opposite sides in the middle of the field. One defender passes the ball into either one of the two attackers. Attackers can score into any goal after making a minimum of 3 in field passes. 3 v 2 with attackers allowed to play unopposed in the channels, defenders cannot enter these areas.

Key Differences: Numbers up situation with an emphasis on positioning, players are encouraged to use width and stretch the defending team. Stress the importance of identifying opportunities and exploiting them.

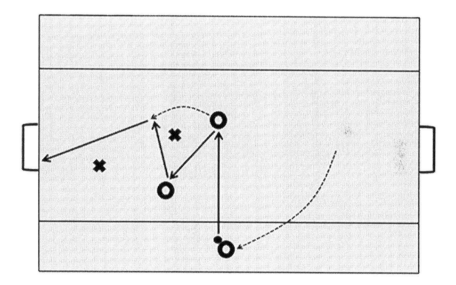

Attacking as a Unit SSG (Alternative 4)

How To: Set up a 50 x 40 yard area with a coned line down the middle of the field. Normal game rules apply however for a goal to count, all players on the attacking team must be standing in the opposition half.

Key Differences: Even if you don't have the ball you still have a duty to support in attack. This places a greater emphasis on moving with your team as a unit for both attack and defense.

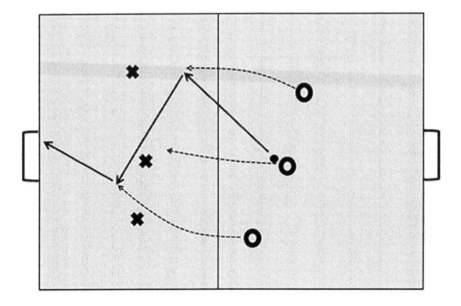

Using Support to Bypass Defenders

SCU Online Reference:
Month 7 Attacking

Month 7-1

Quick Switches and Dribbling

How To: 12-yard square with a player on each corner. 2 players in the middle with a ball each. Players in the middle must dribble towards a player on the outside and make a layoff pass to a player on the outside who must collect the ball and run back to the middle before finding another player on the outside to lay the ball off to.

Coaching Points: Quick movement and decision making, layoff pass and control should be crisp, receiving player should try to control the ball into their path so as not to break their stride. Pass into the path of the player, move at an angle to them to keep the play moving and seamless

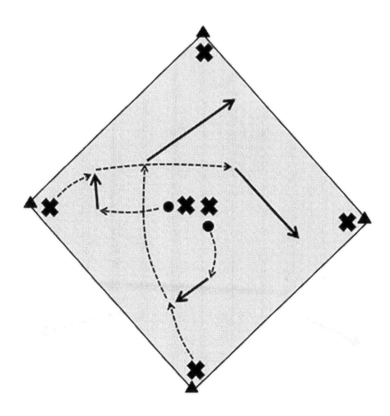

Month 7-2

1 – 2 Patterns with Pressure

How To: 15 x 15-yard area with a player in each corner, 2 players on each the same side have a ball. Player 1 starts off the sequence by passing the ball to the opposite corner and closes down the receiving player, the other free player steps in field to support, the two players must perform a simple give and go under passive pressure. The player receiving the ball runs to the other end, the supporting player becomes the passive defender for the player with the ball in the opposite corner.

Coaching Points: Supporting player must step in closer to support on the blind side of the defender, wide enough to offer a good angle of support for receiving the pass and making the successful return ball.

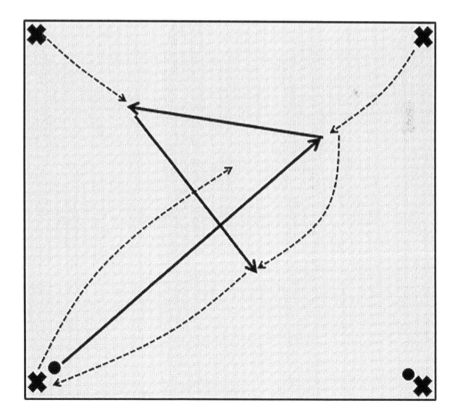

4 v 2- Linking with Wide Players

How To: 2v2 in central area with 2 wide supporting players and an attacker in an end zone. The ball must be passed in field, out to a wide player and back in field before a player can shoot.

Coaching Points: This can be played with several conditions: Pass to the one striker who must shoot- Pass to the lone striker who must make a lay off pass back to the midfielder who takes a shot. Move the ball quickly, take advantage of numerical advantage/overload. Communicate, encourage positive/exaggerated angles of support. Be positive and take chances.

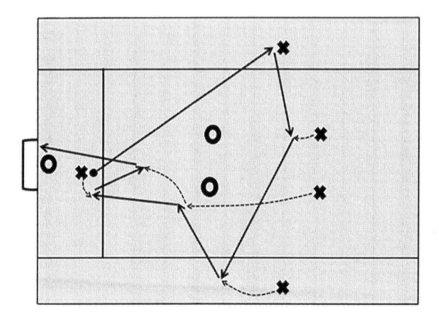

Finishing from Layoffs SSG

How To: 3 v 3 played in a central area with two attacking target players occupying attacking zones as shown in the diagram. Teams must make a number of passes inside the central zone then play a ball into one of their target players. The target player must make a first time lay off for a central player to run onto and shoot first time on goal.

Coaching Points: Weight of pass and layoff is important when striking the ball first time. Get the basic technique right when striking the ball, communicate well and dictate where you would like the layoff, read the game and anticipate play, be positive.

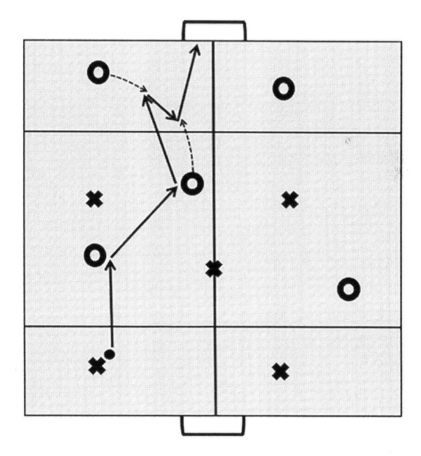

Quick Passing and Moving

How To: 12-yard square with a player on each corner. 2 players in the middle with a ball each. A player in the middle passes to a player on the outside on an angle and moves to receive a pass back, on receiving the return pass the player must look to pass to a new player on the outside.

Key Differences: Bigger emphasis on passing, players should be looking to see which player is free before they receive the ball back so that their first touch can be in the right direction to make the next pass.

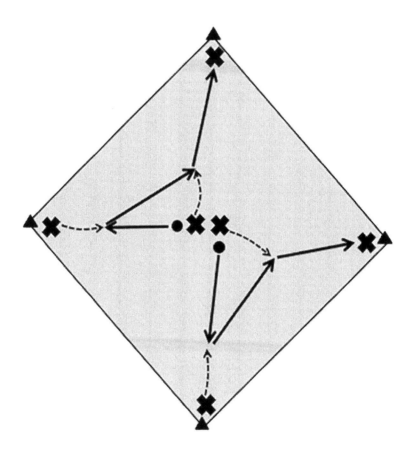

1 – 2's with Pressure

How To: 15 x 15-yard area with a player in each corner, 2 players on each the same side have a ball. Player 1 starts off the sequence by passing the ball to the opposite corner. The player down the line closes down the receiving player, player one must move quickly to support and receive a pass on an angle before dribbling to the free corner.

Key Differences: Supporting player must move quickly to support, getting onside quickly and maintaining a good angle to receive the pass, The defender can close the receiver down quickly and make the pass away difficult, the emphasis is on the supporting player to make up the ground and create the space.

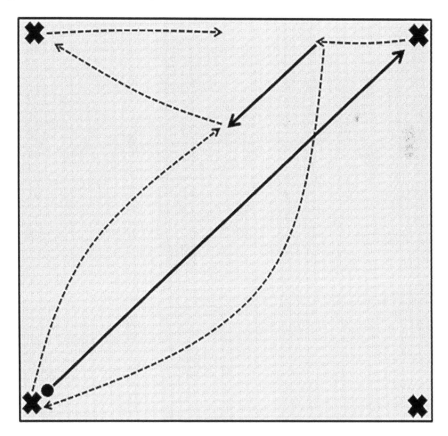

4 v 2- Linking with Wide Players

How To: 2v2 in central area with 2 wide supporting players and an attacker in an end zone. The ball must be passed in field, out to a wide player and back in field before a player can shoot. The final pass must be into the attacker in the end zone who can take a maximum of 2 touches.

Key Differences: The pass into the attacker is now a crucial point too. Attacker in the end zone must be alert to the pass and take a good first touch to set up the shot. Final pass and speed of movement in the end zone are important. Add a defender to increase the difficulty further. End zone attacker can then choose to take the shot themselves or lay off back to the advancing midfielder.

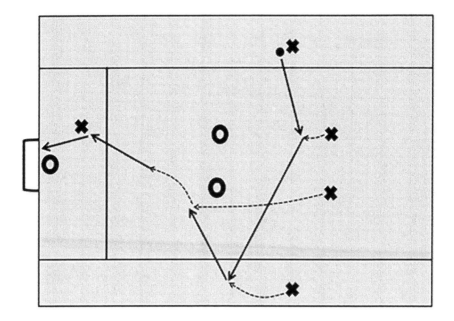

Finishing from Layoffs SSG

How To: 3 v 3 played in a central area with two attacking target players occupying attacking zones as shown in the diagram. Teams must make a number of passes inside the central zone then play a ball into one of their target players. The target player must make a first time lay off to their partner in the next target area before shooting.

Key Differences: Movement of the two end zone attackers should be reactive; I.E when one receives the ball deep, the other should react by dropping off at an angle to receive the layoff to attack first time. If the player receives short, they should react by making a run off them to attack a flick on. Work on communication and understanding.

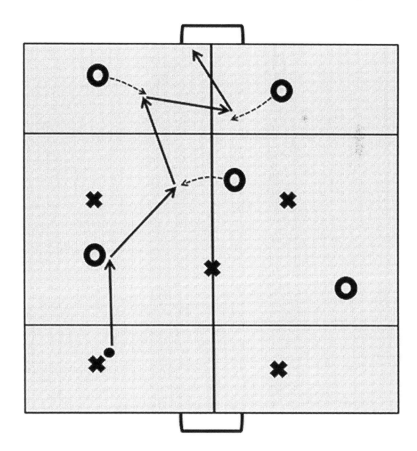

Dribbling - Carrying the Ball Forward

SCU Online Reference:
Month 1 Dribbling

Dribbling Freestyle.

How To: Set out cones randomly in the center of the field. Players work from opposite corners, one ball per side. Both corner players can move at the same time and must dribble freely through the cones before passing off to the player on the other side.

Coaching Points: Dribble with your head up, use different parts of both feet to maneuver through the cones. Challenge yourself by choosing different routes through the cones. Avoid other players who may be dribbling at the same time by constantly checking your surroundings.

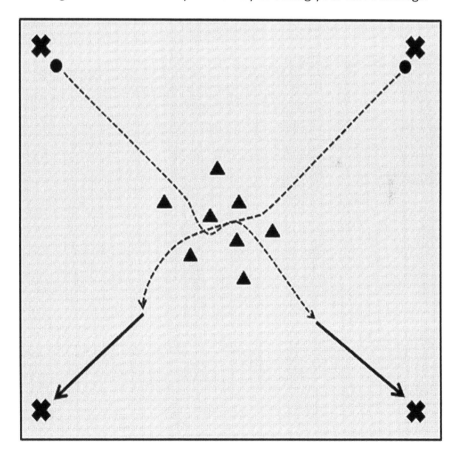

The Gauntlet.

How To: Set a 25 x 15-yard area with three sections. Set 3 defenders along the gauntlet. These defenders can only move side to side along their line. The attacker must dribble from one side of the field to the other, scoring points for each defender they successfully pass.

Coaching Points: Speed of attack, use the space available. Use skills and trickery to move past defenders. Attack at pace and move into space when it is available. Move with your head up and be positive. Keep the ball close when under pressure.

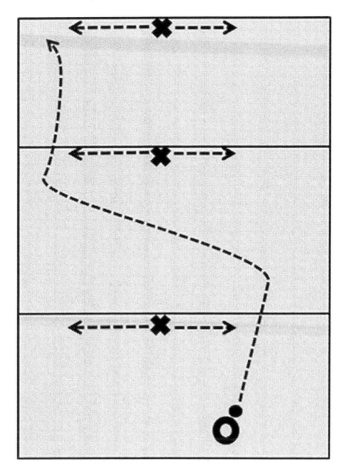

Month 1-3

1 v 1 on First Touch

How To: 30 x 30 Yard area with a cone gate approximately 25 yards from goal (set up the field as shown to avoid lines, adjust the size of the field to accommodate players of differing strength/ability). The first player from the line passes the ball into the player between the cones who controls the ball and attempts to score in the goal they are facing. The player who passes initially becomes the defender.

Coaching Points: Quality of first touch- should take you towards goal into the space. Speed of attack, move into the space available quickly. Attack the defender at speed and take the opportunity when you have created space for a goal scoring opportunity.

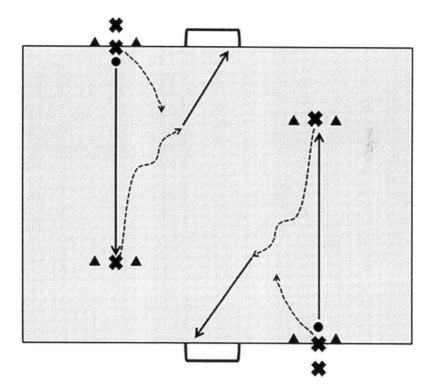

Targets - Dribbling Team Game

How To: 3 v 3 played on a 25 x 30-yard field played width ways. Normal game rules apply. There are three scoring gates on each side of the field. One team defends their side and attacks the other. Points are scored whenever a player dribbles through one of the gates they need to attack.

Coaching Points: Movement with and without the ball. Utilize the space available. Be positive when you have the ball and attack space. Try to take on defenders and commit them to open up space elsewhere on the field. Use your teammates. Differences between dribbling and running with the ball. (using laces when RWB to move faster when space is available, keep the ball closer using different parts of the foot when dribbling).

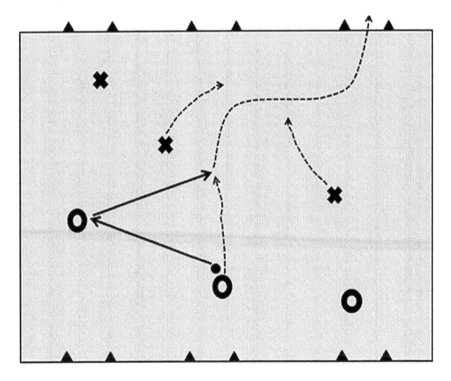

Dribbling in Pairs (Alternative 1)

How To: Players start at opposite ends with a cone between the two of them, they must dribble their ball towards the cone before making a move around the cones then dribble to the other side.

Key Differences: Obstacle is now moving, communicate with your opposite number (verbal and nonverbal)

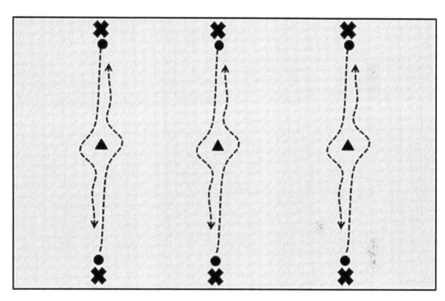

1v1 Dribbling to Gates (Alternative 2)

How To: Attacker and defender start in opposite corners, the defender passes to the attacker who can then dribble through either gate to score a point, defender must try to win the ball back, if they are successful they can score a point by dribbling through either gate.

Key Differences: The defenders are now applying restrictive pressure which is no longer lateral. The attacker has a wider scope of target and bigger field space, this offers more open free play while still maintaining an attacking advantage, encourage creativity and trickery.

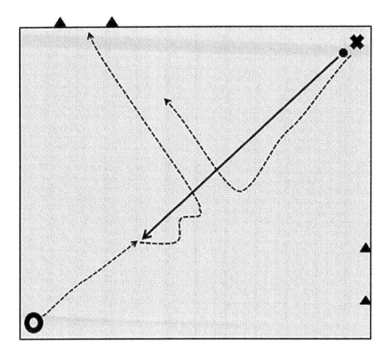

1v1 Challenge (Alternative 3)

How To: Defender passes to the attacker then moves to defend. The attacker scores a point by stopping the ball anywhere on the defenders start line, if the defender wins the ball back they can then try to stop the ball on the attackers start line and score a point.

Key Differences: Sole focus is on the 1v1 element and taking the defender on, removing the goal takes away the temptation to take a shot and forces the player to beat their man.

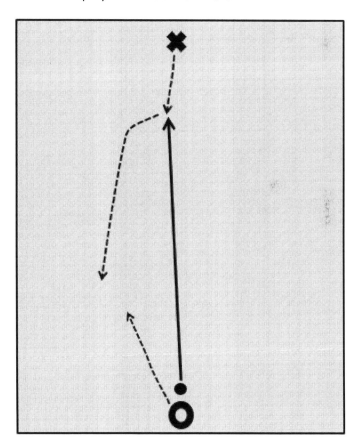

Target - Dribbling SSG (Alternative 4)

How To: Divide the end zones of your field so there are two 8 yard channels before the gated goals. Players can only dribble in these end zones. Small sided game with even teams. The same rules apply as in the normal session plan.

Key Differences: Whereas before, a player could receive the ball and score from anywhere, now when a player dribbles into the coned zone, they cannot pass the ball unless they dribble back into the regular field, this means they are committed to taking on a player and must move quickly as all of the opposing team can help to defend against that one player if they're not quick enough.

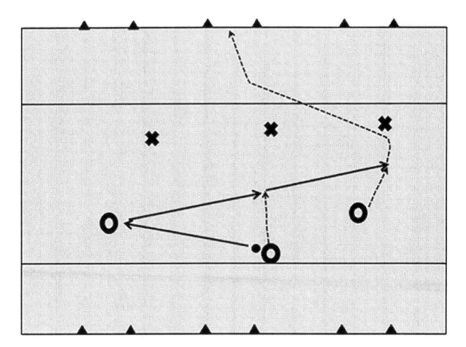

Committing Defenders - Creating Space

SCU Online Reference:
Month 5 Dribbling

Committing the Defender

How To: Set up a 25 x 10 yards area with players lined up at either side, players work in 2's moving from one side to the other, there is a cone in the middle of the field (defender) The player on the ball must dribble at the defender before passing to the supporting player, both players advance to the end.

Coaching Points: Drive into the space near the defender to commit them positionally, once you've committed the defender release the pass. Timing of the pass to create optimum space is crucial. Be positive with both run, support and pass.

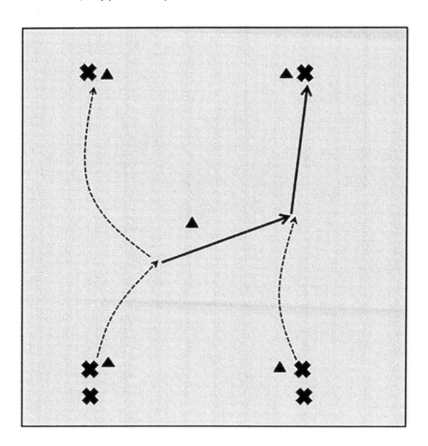

Committing the Defender- Passive Pressure (A2)

How To: Use a 25 x 25-yard square with a goal at either end. One defender occupies a central channel which they cannot move from. Players work in twos to bypass the defender and score (add goalkeeper where necessary.) Dribble at the defender to commit them before passing into space to advance.

Coaching Points: Attack the space around the defender to draw them in and commit them before releasing the pass. Remember to run on after your pass to receive a return pass or react to a saved shot. Timing/weight of pass and positive dribbling are essential.

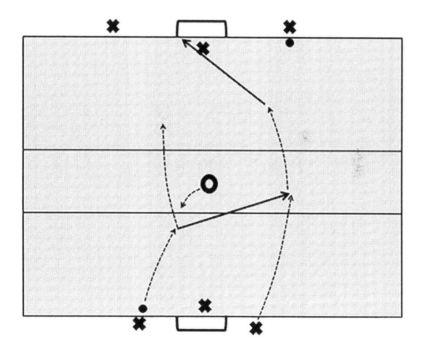

3 v 2 Attacking Waves (A3)

How To: Set up a 25 x 30-yard area with players in groups of 3. 2 Defenders occupy the middle. Players must attempt to move the ball from one side to the other to score a point.

Coaching Points: Take advantage of a numbers up situation, practice running at a defender to commit their position. Players around you must react to the space you're creating and be prepared to move into it. Be creative with runs off the ball. Communication, timing and positive play will all play a part. Attack quickly. Concentrate efforts on dribbling and the space it creates elsewhere on the field.

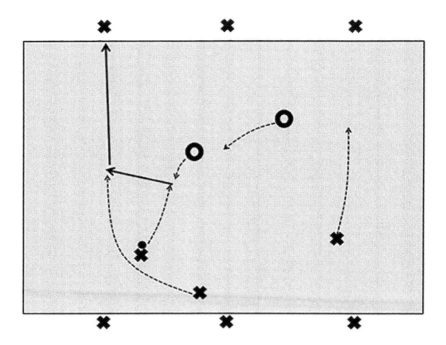

Dribbling End Zones SSG (A4)

How To: 25 x 35-yard field with two small scoring zones at either end. Players play a 3v3 or 4v4 under normal game rules, to score a player must dribble over the end line.

Coaching Points: Create space where possible either by making the field big and spreading out, or maneuvering your opponent. Bonus points if you can commit a defender and release another team mate into space you have created if it leads to a goal. Communication, field awareness, confident dribbling and creativity are all key ingredients for success here.

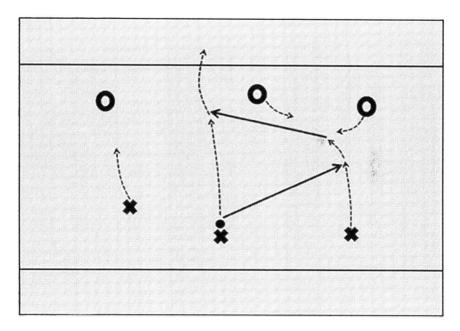

Dribbling and Running with the Ball- Alternative 1

How To: Set up a 25 x 10 yards area with players lined up at either side. Each player at one end has a ball and the field is split into three sections. In the first section players dribble, making as many small touches on the ball as possible while still moving forward, in the middle section they run with the ball at speed, in the final section they take as many small touches as possible before passing to the next player.

Key Differences: Using different parts of the foot to dribble then run, practicing transition from running with the ball using laces to slowing their pace and keeping tighter control when approaching the opposition.

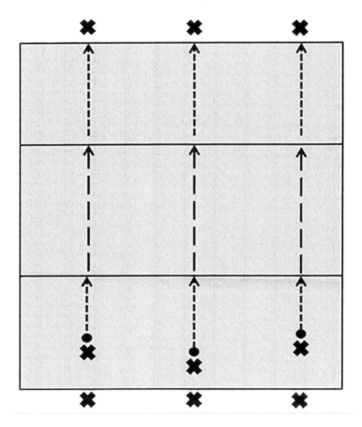

Committing the Defender- Passive Pressure - Alternative

How To: Use a 25 x 25-yard square with a goal at either end. One defender occupies a central channel which they cannot move from. Players work in twos to bypass the defender and score (add goalkeeper where necessary.) Dribble at the defender to commit them before passing into space to advance. The first passing player must receive a return pass then shoot.

Key Differences: The Central channel is larger creating a more even 1v1 situation in the middle area. The First player must now attack the space after drawing the defender.

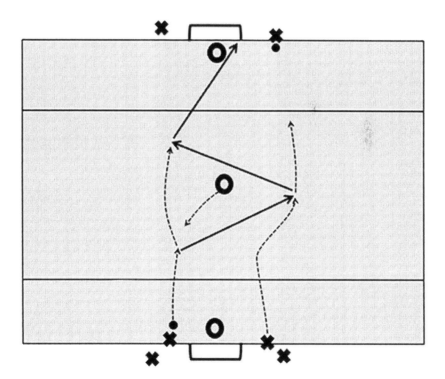

3 v 3 Attacking Waves – Alternative 3

How To: Set up a 25 x 30-yard area with players in groups of 3. 3 Defenders occupy the middle. Players must attempt to move the ball from one side to the other to score a point. Once a point is scored the defenders must all run to the opposite line before moving back into position to defend.

Key Differences: 3v3 in a real pressure scenario. Once a point is scored the defenders must run away from the new wave of attackers and touch the line before defending. The new wave of attackers should look to attack this space quickly to score a quick point. If defenders win the ball they switch roles. Look for quick transitions between attack and defense.

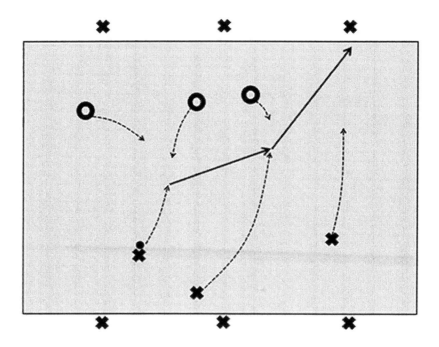

Dribbling End Zones SSG with Gates- Alternative 4

How To: 25 x 35-yard field with two small scoring zones at either end. Players play a 3v3 or 4v4 under normal game rules, to score a player must dribble over the end line through a gate.

Key Differences: Dribbling player must keep their head up and aware of the gate positions. Defenders can defend much easier. As it is an even numbers game there is a greater emphasis on committing a defender and attacking the space it creates quickly.

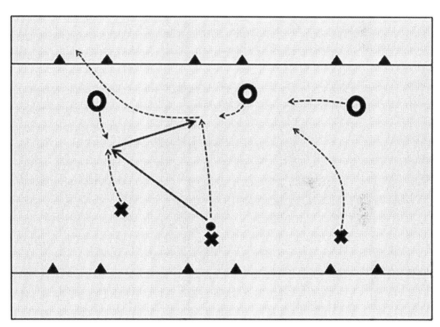

Month 10 Dribbling
- Identifying Space/Decision Making -

SCU Online Reference:
Month 10 Dribbling

Dribbling/Running with the Ball -Warm up

How To: Set up a 30 x 30 yard area with a cone in the middle and a small area in each corner, players work in opposite corners, in this image the top right and bottom left corner players dribble into the middle cone, turn back and pass off to the other player in the corner who moves outside the box to receive the pass. Top left to bottom right is dribbling up to the cone, moving around it and playing a give and go with the player opposite.

Coaching Points: Lengthen stride and push the ball with your laces when running into space, shorten strides when approaching an obstacle using different parts of your foot to control. Move with your head up and be positive.

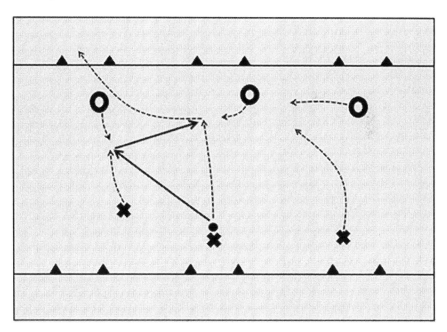

Corners and Space - Unopposed

How To: 35 x 35-yard area with a 5x5 square in the middle. Every player has a ball. Players must dribble their ball into each corner area, returning to the middle area each time before moving to the next corner. Re start and add rules once all players have reached the middle.

Coaching Points: Try this without a ball initially, make it a problem solver. Do you have to be the fastest player to do this? Or can you work out a quicker way? Add a ball and make this a competition. Focus should be keeping the ball under control. Identifying when to dribble with close control and when to run with the ball. Add more players – no more than 2 players in any area at one time (apart from the middle area).

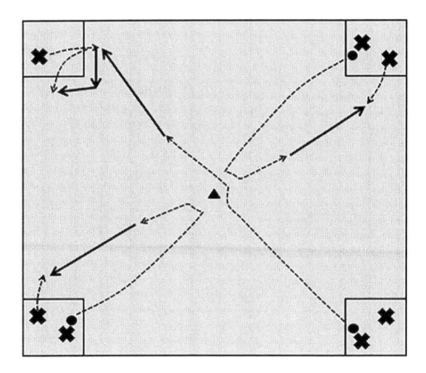

Corners and Spaces – Real Pressure

How To: 35 x 35-yard area with a 5x5 square in the middle. Every player has a ball. Players must dribble their ball into each corner area, returning to the middle area each time before moving to the next corner. Players must get to as many corners as possible within the allotted time while avoiding the defenders. Defenders cannot enter the areas.

Coaching Points: Identify opportunities and threats and move quickly. Remain composed, turn out of trouble and shield the ball when under pressure. Be positive and scan the field for opportunity/threats/space. Don't be afraid to lose the ball, just learn from the situation.

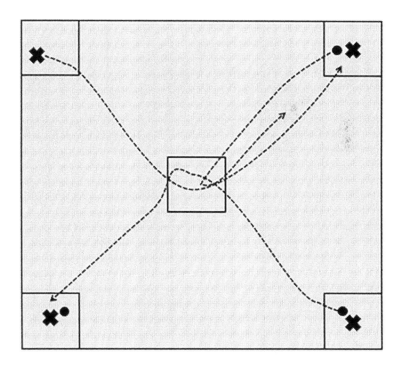

1v1's and Overloads

How To: Set up four 12 x 8-yard areas for 1v1's Play a 2v2 in a 35 x 40 yard central field. If a player wins their 1v1 they join their team in the middle creating a temporary numbers up situation. Only goals scored in the main game count. If you concede in the 1v1 you move to join another 1v1 to make a 2v1. Play the game for 5 minutes, your objective is to get into the main game as quickly as possible to help your team score points.

Coaching Points: Individual technique in the 1v1 both defensively and offensively. Close control and quick, positive play. Identifying space in the main game and exploiting space. Committing defenders to free up team mates and exploiting numerical advantages.

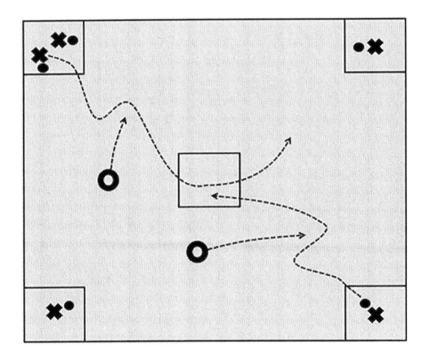

Collect the Colors

How To: Set up a 15 x 15-yard area with 3 players in the middle. Each player wears a colored bib/pinnie and the same colored bib or a cone placed in each corner. Players must collect their cones/bibs one at a time returning each one to the middle before collecting another. No ball required for this warm up.

Key Differences: No soccer ball so players should be completely focused on working out where they need to go and the best route to take. As players are running, players will need to be intelligent to work faster than a quicker runner.

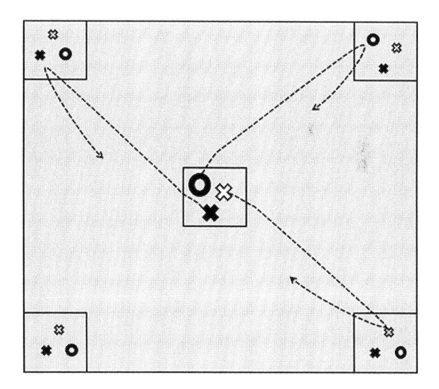

Corners and Space - Unopposed

How To: 35 x 35-yard area with a 5x5 square in the middle. Every player has a ball. One area has been removed. Players must dribble their ball into each corner area, returning to the middle area each time before moving to the next corner. No more than 2 players in any zone at one time apart from the middle area.

Key Differences: As one area has been removed so the area will be more crowded. Players will have to concentrate on where they are moving to and where others are moving to. If they identify an area that doesn't already have two players in they must move to it quickly. You don't have to be the quickest player to win consistently. There is a bigger emphasis on identifying space and working intelligently.

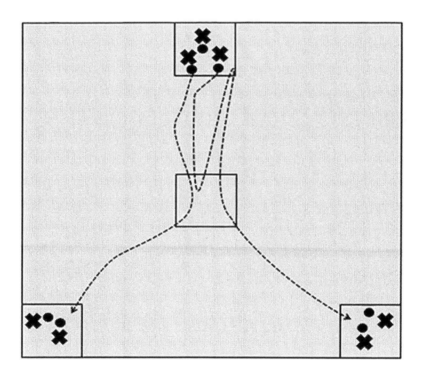

Collect the Colors – Team Play.

How To: Set up a 35 x 35-yard area with a player in each corner each with a ball. (This can also be set up as a relay race with one ball per team.)   Players must dribble their ball to the middle, collect a cone which matches the color of their bib and take it back to their corner.

Key Differences: Moving quickly with good control is a priority. Once all cones are in corners you can change the game to focus on collecting any cone from any other area. Players will have to scan the field for threat and opportunity and react accordingly.

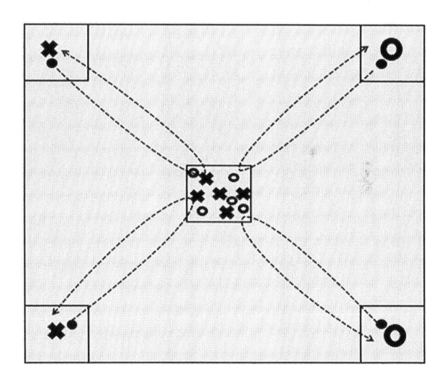

Champions League 1v1's

How To: Set up 8 x 12 channels for 1v1s next to each other. Players start by passing to the player at the opposite end to start play. Re-set if the ball leaves the area. Points are scored by stopping the ball on the opponents end line. Play for a minute, keep a note of who won/lost and change opponents. Keep a mini league table.

Key Differences: 1v1's in a pure form, no targets or goals just repetition of scenarios and testing your skills against different opposition.

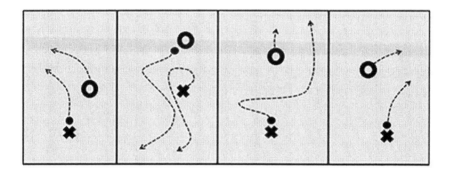

Attack vs Defense
- Problem Solving - Attack vs Defense -

SCU Online Reference:
Month 11 Attack vs Defense

Combination Movement Warm up

How To: Set up a 45 x 30-yard field with a 3-yard coned diamond in the middle and a pop-up goal as shown in the diagram. Give and go and movement warm up. Key pass is in the middle, player steps away from the cone to provide the angle for the overlapping player, pass must go through 2 sides of the triangle. Play a half pressure 1v1 to the pop-up goal. Make sure you move to take the position of the next player each time.

Coaching Points: Passing accuracy, moving at half pace to begin with being sure to incorporate dynamic stretching when moving to the next position to warm up thoroughly. Passing and support angles to open up the field for the next pass.

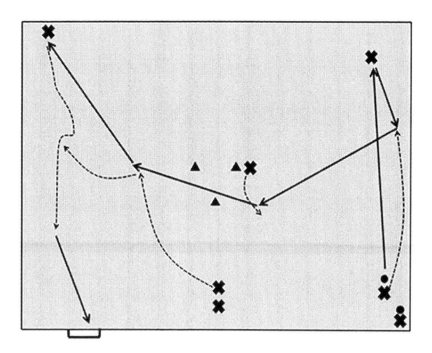

Build up Play and Pass Weight Accessory Work

How To: 35 x 20-yard area with a pop-up goal at either end- a 5 yard gap in the middle occupied by a defender, 2 10 yard areas either side of that and 2 more unoccupied 10 yard no-go zones before the goal. 2 players on one side must work a passing opportunity to the player in the opposite zone. The receiving player makes a first time lay off to the player who passed the ball in who must strike the ball first time before the ball comes to a stop.

Coaching Points: Pass patiently to work an opportunity to pass to your team mate. Try passing to feet and passing to space to draw an opportunity. Communicate clearly with the receiving player who is making the layoff for you to shoot, tell them where you want it played and move onto the ball positively focusing on good shooting technique.

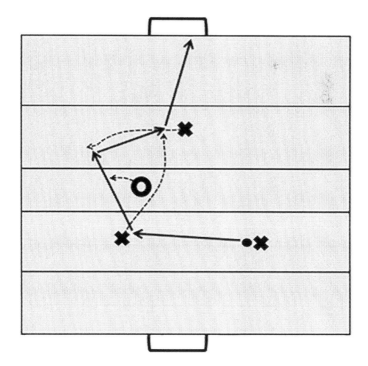

Numbers up Transitions

How To: 40 x 30-yard area (adjust to accommodate more players/adjust based on player age) Play 5v5 or 6v6 in the area. The team in possession plays with the full team, the team without the ball must sacrifice 2 players who must stand on the goal line and can only use their hands. Goals only count if they cross the line below the knee. Placement over power – Safety first!

Coaching Points: Take advantage of the numbers up situation by using all the field space. Stretch the play and identify/capitalize on space when it appears. If you lose the ball you must communicate to get up defensively and get two players on the line as quickly as possible.

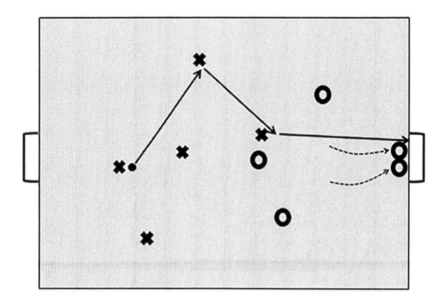

Attack vs Defense -Conditioned Free Play

How To: Use a full-size field with a line down the middle and a line across the final third. Numbers up 8v5. Conditioned journey to the final third. Play a 5 v 3 in one half of the field. The remaining 3 players keep shape for the relief pass. On the other half of the field. After 5 passes, switch the play and try to move towards goal quickly in the space created. Players can move anywhere in the final third but must keep some shape in the other 2 thirds.

Coaching Points: confidence playing out from the back and in a confined space. Awareness to pick out the player in space, pass accuracy and focus. Discipline to play your position in the build up play. Creativity and freedom in the final third.

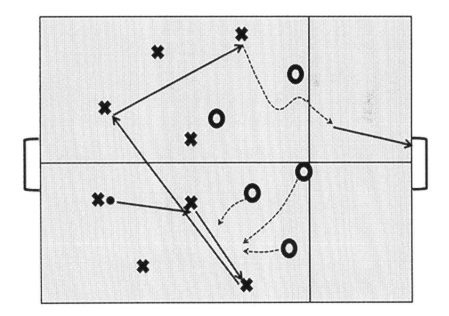

Attack vs Defense - Problem Solving
- Attack vs Defense -

SCU Online Reference:
Month 12 Attack vs Defense

Volleys and Control out of the Air in 2's

How To: In pairs with 1 ball between 2, throw the ball up and control it out of the air, then return the throw to your team mate. Build up to playing 'two touches' one touch to control and one to pass back to your team mate.

Coaching Points: Don't be afraid of the ball, watch the flight, get your feet ready and look to cushion the ball with your foot, thigh or chest. Practice controlling the ball in different directions, directional control will help you find more space in a game.

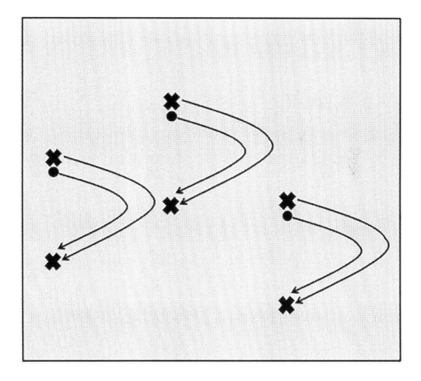

Lofted Passes – Cushioned Touches

How To: 25 x 30 yard area with a line down the middle. A team must make 3 passes then chip the ball into the opposite team. Players must meet the ball before it bounces and try to control the ball into the path of their teammate.

Coaching Points: Be alert to the flight of the ball. Communicate quickly so your teammates know who is controlling the ball. Move close to support and control the cushioned touch in your direction. Floated cross field balls can invite pressure where the receiving player is so it is important that you support around the receiver. Quick passes and good quality lofted passes are essential to give both teams a chance at success. Imagine switching play with a cross field ball in a game situation, when and where might you use this?

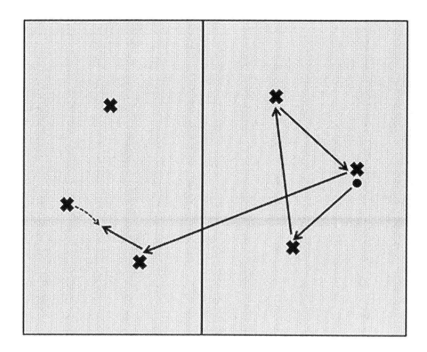

Targets Under Pressure

How To: Set up a 60 x 40 yard area with two larger areas in the middle (20 yards each) and a 10 yard zone at either end. Blues are targeting the two team mates at the far end. Make 4 passes then play a chipped pass into your team mate. If a team mate successfully controls the ball they score a point then pass the ball to the red team. A player from the red zone in the middle and the red end zone can pressure the ball while it is with the blues making a 3v2 (adjust this rule based on success)

Coaching Points: Target men have a marking player- move to create space and read the flight of the ball. Communicate. Teams must read the play, don't force the pass over the top, your team mate may have a better passing angle. Control the ball without it bouncing to score a point. When controlling from the air, adjust your body to suit the delivery. Cushioned touches work to bring the ball under control. Make sure you are controlling the ball into good space away from the oncoming defender.

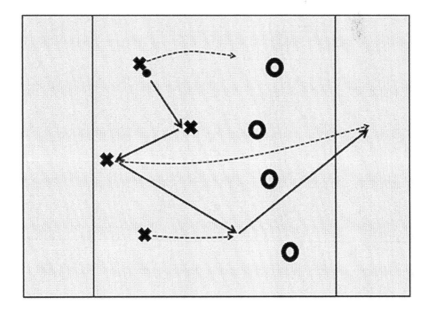

Target men SSG

How To: Free play 6v6 with 2 end zones (3v3 in central area, 1v1 in each end zone and a goalkeeper) Players look to work a lofted pass into the target player. A team mate from the middle can then move into the end zone to support in a 2v1 or the target man can try to score by themselves. The ball must be controlled first time out of the air but allow for 1 bounce if the pass is good.

Coaching Points: Target man should be alert and aware, creating space and being available for the ball in. Use your body to hold the ball up and focus on a good first touch. Good target players will be able to identify support runs and flick the ball into their path. The midfield players should be scanning the field for opportunity and being patient. You can pass back to your defender or keeper to recycle possession and change the angle of attack.

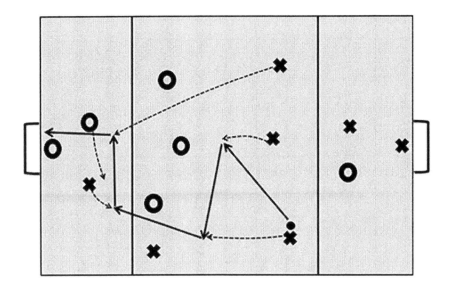

Through Balls in 3's

How To: Two players start on a cone each 15 yards apart with 1 middle 'runner'. The runner starts with the ball, dribbling towards an end player and passing into their feet, the runner must then run behind the receiver to simulate an overlap and receive a through ball into their path.

Coaching Points: communicate with the player in possession as you're approaching from their blind side, let them know when they should release the pass. Weight of pass needs to be into the path of the runner so they can control the ball in their stride without slowing their run. Timing, weight of pass and communication are important here..

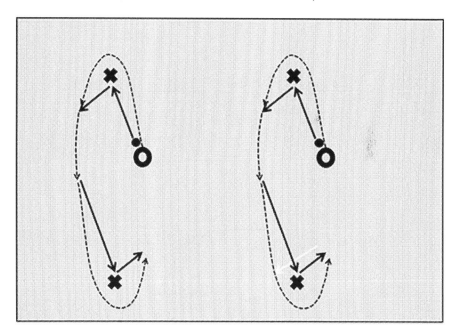

Connecting Midfielders and Forwards

How To: Set up a 50 x 30 yard area with a 3 yard channel across the middle. 3 players start on one side with a ball and two on the other side without a ball. A defender occupies each zone and the middle channel. The team of 3 must make 3 passes then play a through ball to one of their players running into the other zone in turn becoming a team of 2. The team of 3 continue the pattern on the other side. Defenders can pressure and the middle channel defender must screen against the through ball..

Coaching Points: The players on the opposite side have an important role to play without the ball, they must move to be available to support once the through pass is played. Be positive, be patient, try to keep the game fast paced.

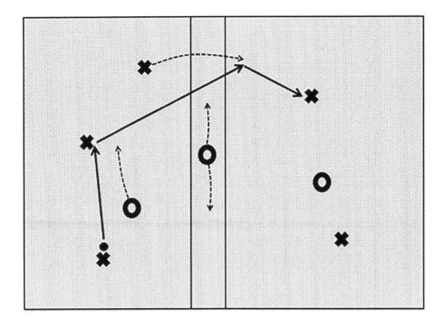

Through Balls Conditioned SSG

How To: 4v4 inside a 50 x 40 main area with a 10-yard end zone on either end. Play as a numbers up game initially to increase success rates if necessary. Teams Play under normal game rules but must pass a through ball to a teammate which is controlled in the end zone in order to score a point. The line of the end zone counts as the last defender so if you're in the end zone before the ball is played you're offside.

Coaching Points: Positive movement, be patient with build up play and consider your pass. A good run off the ball may draw defenders away from a key area. Focus on runs off runs and attack space. Finally, always consider the weight of pass and technique. Be spatially aware with and without the ball.

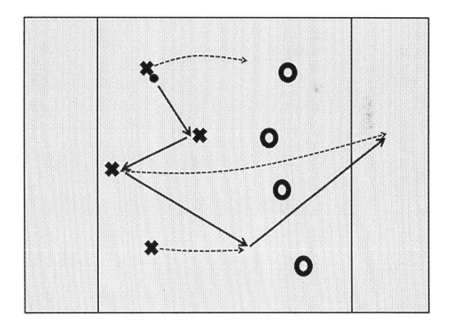

Small Sided Game – Free play

How To: Set up a small sided game with even teams – Let them play!

Coaching Points: recap some of the work on attacking and the different scenarios created. Players have been thrown into different attacking scenarios. Encourage players to solve the problems by going around the sides, over the top or through the middle of their opposition, reminding them that you may have to combine two attacking styles to create a chance- for example: passing wide to stretch the opposition before coming back in field and playing through the middle into the gaps you have created.. Praise successful, fluid attacks and recap where necessary, but try to let the game flow with limited input, let them test what they are learning in a safe, pressure free learning environment.

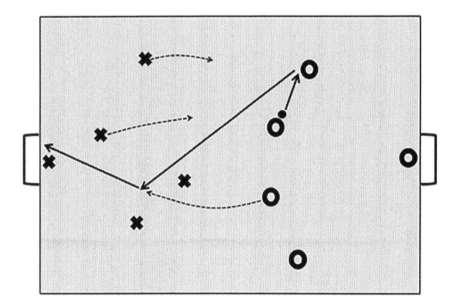

ABOUT COACHES TRAINING ROOM

Coaches Training Room was founded in 2014 and provides beginner, intermediate and advanced coaches with soccer video sessions, PDF downloads, webinars, articles, books and more!

"I am a coach because of the kids and the passion I have for the sport itself. There is no other feeling quite like helping young athletes further develop their natural persistence, determination, discipline, dedication, resilience, work ethic, heart, leadership skills, connection with, and respect for others, not only in competition, but in life!" -Coach Mahoe

For More Resources By Coaches Training Room Visit:

www.CoachesTrainingRoom.com

Come Join Us On:
Facebook.com/coachestrainingroom
Twitter.com/coachestrngroom
Instagram.com/coachestrainingroom

When sharing our content on social media please use HASHTAG:
#CoachesTrainingRoom

Contact Us:
info@coachestrainingroom.com
801-810-4423

www.coachestrainingroom.com

Made in the USA
Middletown, DE
14 August 2018